Abby and the Enchanted Willow

A Story of Friendship and Acceptance

Ellen Elbe Jones

Copyright © Ellen Elbe Jones 2024

All Rights Reserved

No part of this publication may be reproduced, distributed, or transmitted in any form or by any means, including photocopying, recording, or other electronic or mechanical methods, without the author's prior written permission, except in the case of brief quotations embodied in critical reviews and certain other non-commercial uses permitted by copyright law. For permission requests, please get in touch with the author.

Dedication

In memory of Amos and Banjo, who loved me unconditionally.

This book is dedicated to all those who feel alone, out of place, or as if they don't belong.

Acknowledgments

I want to acknowledge all of my wonderful friends who encouraged, supported, and assisted me along the way. I especially want to thank Amanda Sayewich, who provided her artistic perspective with each illustration; Suzanne Brandt, for her creative eye; Sharron Luttrell, for her wisdom and editing skills; Cindy Jones and Stephen Fleischer, for cheering me on; and Ann and Ken Wynn, for their enduring friendship.

About the Author

First-time author Ellen Elbe Jones is excited to share a story that came to her as she sat on a riverbank in Arizona. It remained in her journal until she felt it was time to share it with the world. The story is not so different from her own; Ellen has always felt a deep affinity for trees, birds, and animals—being among them is where she feels most at peace. Having spent much of her childhood alone, she hopes Abby's story brings comfort to other children, or even adults, who feel like they don't fit in.

Lonesome Abby sat in her room all day,

Wishing and hoping only to play.

She had no friends, and so she cried

And spent all of her time alone inside.

She wasn't real pretty. She wasn't real smart.

She wasn't so good at sports or at art.

Her teeth were crooked; she was way too thin.

And try as she might, she just couldn't fit in.

When others were mean, she always stayed kind,

Hoping one day a friend she would find.

"I am your friend," her little cat purred.

But she did not hear him, not even a word.

"I don't understand—how can this be?

There must be something wrong with me!

I do not like myself at all.

I wish I were different and not so tall.

Maybe then they'd like me more,"

She cried as she walked out the door.

She wandered to a nearby park,

Walking the path before it got dark.

As she passed beneath a willow tree,

A friendly voice said, "Come sit with me!"

It took her a moment to get over the shock.

She didn't know that trees could talk!

Abby could hardly believe her ears,

But she sat right down and dried her tears.

"There is no need to make a fuss.

You can come and be with us!

For we see the beautiful girl you are.

Your heart shines like the brightest star.

You are so special and full of love—

A beautiful gift from heaven above."

The bird on the branch then sang her a song,

Inviting her to hum along.

The spider nearby said, "I know how you feel.

When anyone sees me, they squeal.

And then they run away and hide,

Making me so sad inside.

But my friends out here like me just the same,

And we're so happy that you came!"

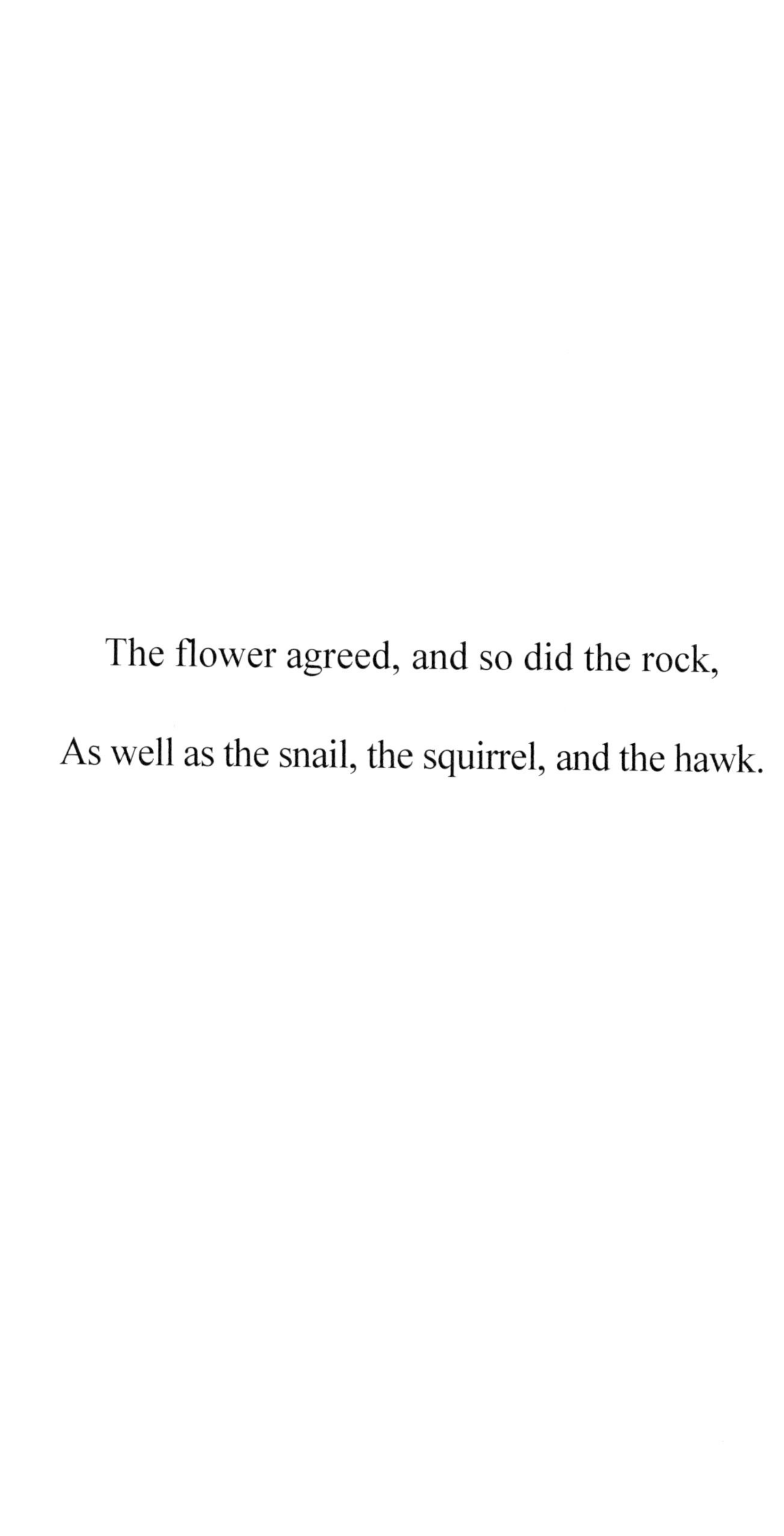

The flower agreed, and so did the rock,

As well as the snail, the squirrel, and the hawk.

"You are always welcome here, so you see,

You have nothing to fear.

Always be happy with who you are,

And you will have friends both near and far."

www.ingramcontent.com/pod-product-compliance
Lightning Source LLC
Chambersburg PA
CBRC100832110726
48006CB00008B/1372